CW00740669

Rod Stewart

Rod Stewart

LIVE | PRIVATE | BACKSTAGE – PHOTOS 1970-1980

PHOTOS: WOLFGANG »BUBI« HEILEMANN

Text: Bubi Heilemann & Sabine Thomas

SCHWARZKOPF & SCHWARZKOPF

INHALTSVERZEICHNIS

CONTENTS

»Every Picture Tells A Story ...«

(ROD STEWART)

Rod Stewarts Autogramm für Bubi – Rod Stewarts Autograph for Bubi. (© WEA-Music)

BUBI HEILEMANN:
DA YA THINK HE'S SEXY?

Als ich Rod Stewart Anfang der siebziger Jahre zum ersten Mal in London traf, ahnte ich nicht, dass aus dem hageren Sänger mit der krächzenden Reibeisenstimme einer der größten Rockstars aller Zeiten werden sollte. Rod Stewart ist immer noch sehr sexy – auch heute zu seinem 60. Geburtstag am 10. Januar 2005 macht er seinem Spitznamen »Hot Rod« alle Ehre!

Genau 25 Jahre nach seinem weltweiten Nummer-Eins-Album »Blondes Have More Fun« führt Rod wieder die US-Charts an. Während meiner Vorbereitung zu diesem Bildband im Herbst 2004 schoss er mit dem Album »The Great American Songbook Vol. III« von Null auf Platz eins der amerikanischen Billboard-Charts – das hat vor ihm noch nie ein Künstler geschafft!

Rod Stewart ist ein Phänomen. Der »Sweet Little Rock'n'Roller« hat im Laufe seiner unglaublichen Karriere über 130 Mio. Platten weltweit verkauft, seine Alben wurden mit unzähligen Silber-, Gold- und Platinauszeichnungen überschüttet. Seit über 30 Jahren stürmt er regelmäßig die Charts und begeistert seine Fans immer wieder aufs Neue. Mit Songs wie »Maggie May«, »Sailing« oder »Hot Legs« hat er Evergreens geschrieben. 13 Mal war er für den Grammy nominiert, bereits 1994 wurde er mit dem American Music Award für sein Lebenswerk ausgezeichnet und in die legendäre Rock and Roll Hall of Fame aufgenommen. Was für eine Karriere – vom Totengräber zum Superstar!

Wenn ich in meinem Foto-Archiv wühle, fällt mir immer wieder auf: Der Zahn der Zeit nagt nicht nur an mir, sondern auch an den Stars, die ich als Exklusiv-Fotograf der damals größten europäischen Jugendzeitschrift BRAVO in den Sechzigern und Siebzigern vor der Linse hatte. Viele von ihnen sind inzwischen im Rock'n'Roll Himmel: John Lennon und George Harrison, Jimi Hendrix und Janis Joplin, Marc Bolan und Mickey Finn von T. Rex, um nur einige zu nennen. An Rod Stewart jedoch scheint die wilde Zeit beinahe spurlos vorübergegangen zu sein. Ich finde sogar, er sieht heute besser aus denn je. Er ist eben wie guter Wein: je älter, desto besser. Happy Birthday, Rod!

Wolfgang »Bubi« Heilemann

BUBI HEILEMANN:
DA YA THINK HE'S SEXY?

I first met Rod Stewart in London in the early 70s, and little did I know that this gaunt singer with the scratchy voice was to become one of the greatest rock stars of all time. Rod Stewart is still sexy even today – he'll be 60 on January 10th 2005 and still true to his nickname: »Hot Rod.«

Exactly 25 years after his worldwide number one album »Blondes Have More Fun,« Rod is topping the US charts once again. While I was putting this book together in the fall of 2004, he went from zero to number one on the US Billboard Charts with his album »The Great American Songbook Vol. III« – no other artist has ever managed that!

Rod Stewart is a phenomenon. This »Sweet Little Rock'n'Roller« has sold over 130 million records worldwide during the course of his incredible career. His albums have been showered with silver, gold and platinum awards too numerous to count. He's been regularly storming the charts and thrilling his fans time and again for over 30 years. Songs like »Maggie May,« »Sailing« and »Hot Legs« have become classics. He's been nominated 13 times for a Grammy, in 1994 the American Music Awards honored him for his lifework, and he was admitted into the legendary Rock and Roll Hall of Fame. What a career – from gravedigger to superstar!

I was the exclusive photographer in the sixties and seventies photographing the stars for BRAVO, Europe's most popular youth magazine at the time, and whenever I rummage around in my photo archives I can't help but notice that I'm not the only one who hasn't withstood the ravages of time. Many of those rock stars are already in rock'n'roll heaven: John Lennon and George Harrison, Jimi Hendrix and Janis Joplin, Marc Bolan and Mickey Finn of T. Rex, just to name a few. But it almost seems as if those early days of abandon have left no trace on Rod Stewart. I think he looks even better today than he did then.

He's like a good wine: the older, the better. Happy Birthday, Rod!

Wolfgang »Bubi« Heilemann

STECKBRIEF / BIOGRAPHY
ROD STEWART

NAME: Roderick David Stewart
GEBURTSDATUM: 10. Januar 1945
GEBURTSORT: London
ELTERN: Elsie und Robert Stewart
  (beide schottischer Herkunft)
GESCHWISTER: Don, Bob, Mary, Peggy
EHEN: Verheiratet mit Alana Hamilton von 1979 bis 1984
  und mit Rachel Hunter von 1990 bis 1999
KINDER: Sarah (*1965), Kimberley (*21.8.79),
  Sean (*1.9.80), Ruby (*17.6.87),
  Renee (*1.6.92), Liam McAllister (*6.9.94)

NAME: Roderick David Stewart
DATE OF BIRTH: 10. January 1945
PLACE OF BIRTH: London
PARENTS: Elsie and Robert Stewart
  (both of Scottish descent)
SIBLINGS: Don, Bob, Mary, and Peggy
MARRIAGES: Married to Alana Hamilton from 1979
  to 1984, and to Rachel Hunter from 1990 to 1999
CHILDREN: Sarah (born 1965), Kimberley (born Aug. 21st
  1979), Sean (born Sept. 1st 1980), Ruby (born June 17th
  1987), Renee (born June 1st 1992), Liam McAllister
  (born Sept. 6th 1994)

WERDEGANG:

Mit 16 Jahren verließ Rod die Schule und unterschrieb einen Vertrag beim Londoner Brentford Football Club. Seine Karriere als zukünftiger Fußballstar dauerte allerdings nur drei Wochen, dann entschied er sich für die Musik. Nebenbei jobbte Rod unter anderem als Schildermaler, Zeitungsausträger und Totengräber. Als Straßenmusiker trampte er durch Spanien und Frankreich, bis er von der französischen Polizei aufgegabelt und ausgewiesen wurde. Mit verschiedenen Bands tingelte er durch britische Folk- und Blues-Clubs. 1964 erschien seine erste Solo-Single mit dem Titel »Good Morning Little Schoolgirl«. 1967 stieg Rod bei der Jeff Beck Group ein. Dort traf er Gitarrist Ron Wood, mit dem er Ende 1969 gemeinsam zu den Small Faces wechselte. Der Rest ist History ...

PROFESSIONAL BACKGROUND:

Rod dropped out of school at 16 to sign a contract with the Brendford Football Club in London. His career as a promising football star however only lasted three weeks – he then decided to turn to music. Rod took on various types of work such as sign maker, newspaper delivery boy and gravedigger. He hitchhiked through Spain and France and played street music for money until the French police picked him up and deported him. As a member in a number of different bands he gigged in cheap British folk and blues clubs. His first solo single came out in 1964 titled »Good Morning Little Schoolgirl.« In 1967 he joined the Jeff Beck Group. That's where he met guitarist Ron Wood with whom he joined the Small Faces in 1969. And the rest is history...

ROD STEWART
UND DIE FACES

Meine erste Begegnung mit Rod Stewart fand in London im Büro von Manager Andrew Oldham statt, den ich schon seit Anfang der sechziger Jahre kannte, als er noch als Pressesprecher für die Beatles und als Manager und Produzent für die Rolling Stones tätig war. Inzwischen besaß Oldham ein eigenes Plattenlabel namens »Immediate« und hatte diverse Künstler unter Vertrag, darunter Marianne Faithfull, Nice, Humble Pie, Donovan und die Small Faces. Als Rod Stewart und ein gewisser Ron Wood von der Jeff Beck Group Ende '69 bei den Small Faces einstiegen, nannte sich die Band von da an schlicht und einfach nur noch »The Faces«.

Mein erster Eindruck von Rod: ein ziemlich hagerer, blasser Typ, dessen Gesicht mich an eine Spitzmaus erinnerte. Seine Stimme klang wie ein rostiges Reibeisen, aber er hatte das gewisse Etwas, das man braucht, um als Popstar Karriere zu machen: Charisma.

Nach einem kurzen Interview begleitete ich die Band zu ihrem Gig ins »Rainbow« – damals einer der angesagtesten Clubs in London. Auf der Leinwand des ehemaligen Kinos liefen während des Konzerts psychedelische Projektionen, die heute auf jedem PC im Windows Media Player mitgeliefert werden, aber damals eine absolute Sensation waren.

Die eigentliche Sensation des Abends war jedoch Rod Stewart. Seine unverwechselbare Stimme, die man sofort unter Tausenden heraushört, ging mir richtig unter die Haut. Er wirbelte quer über die Bühne wie ein Derwisch, und das bedeutete für mich als Fotograf Schwerstarbeit. Denn zu dieser Zeit gab es noch keine superschnellen Motorkameras mit Auto-Focus und Zeit-Belichtungsautomatik, so dass ich Mühe hatte, ihn mit meiner Kamera zu verfolgen, das Objektiv scharf zu stellen, Blende und Zeit einzustellen, den Film schnell manuell weiterzutransportieren und im richtigen Moment den Auslöser zu drücken ...

THE FACES: Rod Stewart (Gesang), Ron Wood (Gitarre), Kenny Jones (Schlagzeug), Ian McLagan (Klavier), Ronnie Lane (Bass)

ROD STEWART
AND THE FACES

I first encountered Rod Steward in Andrew Oldham's (the band's manager) London office, whom I'd known since the beginning of the sixties when he was still the Beatles' spokesman for the press and the Rolling Stones' manager and producer. In the meantime Oldham had his own label called »Immediate« and various artists under contract including Marianne Faithfull, Nice, Humble Pie, Donovan, and the Small Faces. When Rod Stewart and a certain Ron Wood of the Jeff Beck Group joined the Small Faces in 1969, the band called themselves from then on simply »The Faces.«

My first impression of Rod: An extremely gaunt and pale chap whose face reminded me of a shrew mouse. His voice sounded like a rusty grate, but he had that certain something that one would need to make it as a pop star: charisma.

After a short interview I accompanied the band to their gig at the »Rainbow« – one of the hippest clubs in London at the time. An ex-cinema, psychedelic imagery was projected onto the large screen in the background during the concert. Today it comes with every Windows Media Player, but at the time it was an absolute sensation.

But the real sensation of the evening was Rod Stewart. That unmistakable voice that you could have picked out of a crowd really got under my skin. He whirled around all over the stage with the abandonment of a dervish, and me being a photographer, that meant some pretty hard work. At the time there was no super fast motorized cameras with automatic focus and automatic time and exposure, so I had a hard time following him with my camera all the while focusing the lens, setting the time and exposure, manually advancing the film and activating the shutter all at the right moment...

THE FACES: Rod Stewart (vocals); Ron Wood (guitar); Kenny Jones (drums); Ian McLagan (piano); Ronnie Lane (bass)

ES IST NICHT ALLES GOLD, WAS GLÄNZT ...

Während die Faces im Frühjahr 1970 ihre erste LP mit dem Titel »First Step« herausbrachten, führte Rod gewissermaßen ein »Doppelleben« und veröffentlichte weiterhin nebenbei seine Soloplatten. Im Juli '71 erschien sein bereits drittes Solo-Album »Every Picture Tells A Story«, aus dem die Single »Reason To Believe« ausgekoppelt wurde. Eines Tages legte ein Radio-DJ versehentlich die B-Seite der Single auf und sorgte damit für einen Welthit: »Maggie May« stürmte weltweit die Charts, Rod führte als erster Künstler überhaupt gleichzeitig die Album- und Single-Charts in Großbritannien und den USA an.

Im November '71 sollte Rod Stewart seine ersten Silbernen und Goldenen Schallplatten für das Album »Every Picture Tells A Story« und die Hitsingle »Maggie May« erhalten. Die Plattenfirma Philips/Mercury mit Sitz in Holland hatte die Presse hierfür nach Amsterdam in einen kleinen Club eingeladen, und so flog auch ich mit meiner Kamera extra zur Pressekonferenz ein. Vor Ort erfuhr ich, dass wir lediglich während der Pressekonferenz fotografieren durften. Das hieß: Alle Hundert anwesenden Fotografen bekamen dasselbe Motiv vor die Linse. Ich wollte wenigstens ein Motiv, das kein anderer hatte!

Viel Zeit blieb allerdings nicht mehr, um etwas zu arrangieren. Ich schickte meinen Assistenten los, um einen Stapel stinknormale Langspielplatten und eine Dose goldenen Sprühlack zu besorgen, und zwar schnell. Die Zeit drängte. Es war natürlich nicht so einfach, in einer fremden Stadt einen Laden zu finden, der Goldlack im Sortiment hatte! Ich wartete währenddessen ungeduldig vor der Diskothek und musste mich langsam entscheiden, ob ich auf meinen Assistenten warten oder mir doch einen guten Platz bei der Pressekonferenz sichern sollte. Ich wurde ziemlich nervös, als die Türen geöffnet wurden und alle Fotografen in die Disco stürmten, um die besten Plätze vor der Mini-Bühne zu ergattern. Ich entschied mich, noch fünf Minuten zu warten. Nervös blickte ich immer wieder auf die Uhr. Wo blieb nur mein Assistent?

Kurz vor Beginn der Pressekonferenz raste plötzlich ein Taxi um die Ecke, mein Assi sprang atemlos heraus und wedelte triumphierend mit den LPs und einer Dose Goldlack. Sofort rissen wir die Hüllen von den Platten, verteilten die Scheiben auf dem Rasen vor der Disco und sprühten wie wild drauflos. In diesem Moment glitt eine schwarze Limousine mit verdunkelten Scheiben heran, Rod Stewart stieg aus, blieb wie angewurzelt stehen und rief enttäuscht: »Oh! THAT'S how it's done!«

Tatsächlich dachte er einen Schreckensmoment lang, dass wir gerade die Goldenen Schallplatten produzierten, die er wenige Minuten später im Rahmen der Pressekonferenz erhalten sollte! Umso mehr war er erleichtert, als ich den Irrtum aufklärte und ihn bei der Gelegenheit gleich um ein Exklusiv-Foto bat. Nach der offiziellen Verleihung der »richtigen« Goldenen Schallplatte, wo er von Hunderten von Journalisten und Fotografen umringt wurde, löste er sein Versprechen tatsächlich ein und posierte extra für mich mit den zehn »getürkten« goldenen Platten, die wir zuvor besprüht hatten und die er auch noch signierte. Er witzelte: »Es ist nicht alles Gold, was glänzt!«

ALL THAT GLITTERS
IS NOT GOLD...

At the same time the Faces brought out their first LP titled »First Step« in the spring of 1970, Rod led a bit of a double life by continuing to bring out solo records on the side. His third solo album »Every Picture Tells A Story« with the single »Reason To Believe« was released in July of 1971. One day a radio DJ mistakenly played the B-side of the record, which consequently became a worldwide hit. »Maggie May« stormed the charts and Rod was the first artist ever to single-handedly top the album and singles charts in Great Britain and the USA.

In November of 1971 Rod Stewart received his first silver and gold records for the LP »Every Picture Tells A Story« and the hit single »Maggie May.« The headquartered in Holland Phillips/Mercury record company invited the press to a little club in Amsterdam, so I flew in with my camera just for the press conference. When I was there I found out we were only allowed to shoot photos during the press conference. That meant that the one hundred photographers present all would get the same pictures. I wanted at least one image that no one else had!

However, there wasn't a whole lot of time to arrange anything. I sent my assistant to get a stack of totally normal LP records and a can of gold spray paint, and fast – time was running out. It was not easy to find a shop in a foreign city that sold gold paint! Meanwhile I waited impatiently in front of the club and had to decide if I was to wait for my assistant or to go inside to get a good seat for the press conference. I was getting extremely nervous when the doors opened and all the photographers stormed into the club to get the best places up front at the mini-stage. I decided to wait another five minutes. I nervously looked at my watch. Where could my assistant be?

Right before the press conference started a taxi screeched around the corner and my assistant jumped out, totally out of breath, and triumphantly held up the LPs and a can of gold paint. We immediately ripped the records out of their sleeves, spread them out on the grass in front of the club and started spraying like mad. Just at that moment a black limousine with darkened windows glided to a stop. Rod Stewart climbed out, stood rooted to the spot and cried out with disappointment, »Oh! THAT'S how it's done!«

He actually thought for one horrible second that we were producing the gold record that he would be receiving in a few minutes at the press conference! He was that much more relieved when I explained everything and used the opportunity to ask him for an exclusive photo. After the official awarding of the »real« gold record during which he was surrounded by hundreds of journalists and photographers, he made good his promise and posed exclusively for me with the ten »fake« gold records that we had just sprayed. He even signed them all and joked, »All that glitters is not gold!«

DER MANN MIT
DEN ZWEI GESICHTERN

Nachdem Rod Stewart innerhalb kürzester Zeit zum Superstar avancierte, gerieten die Faces immer mehr in den Hintergrund und wurden bei gemeinsamen Konzerten praktisch zu Rods Begleitband degradiert. Rod stand stets im Mittelpunkt des Geschehens, im Focus der Medien und der Fans. Auch gab es zunehmend musikalische Differenzen. Rod plädierte dafür, mehr Balladen ins Repertoire aufzunehmen, die anderen wollten lieber härtere Töne anschlagen. Ronnie Lane spielte mit dem Gedanken, die Band zu verlassen, und Ronnie Wood flirtete bereits kräftig mit den Rolling Stones.

Im April '73 brachten die Faces ihr viertes Album mit dem Titel »Ooh La La« heraus, kurz darauf machte Ronnie Lane seine Drohung wahr und verließ die Band. Als Ersatz für ihn kam der Japaner Tetsu Yamouchi, der früher bei Free gespielt hatte. Tetsu brachte wieder frischen Wind in die Band, und auch Rod versprach, sich wieder mehr in die Band zu integrieren und seine Solo-Ambitionen deutlicher von den Faces zu trennen. Er bekannte sich zu seinen »zwei Gesichtern« – auf der einen Seite der harte Rock'n'Roller, auf der anderen Seite der romantische Schmusebarde.

Nach Tetsus Einstieg planten die Faces eine große Welt-Tournee, die sie nach Australien, Neuseeland, Japan und Europa führen sollte. Zum Auftakt der Tour flog ich im Dezember '73 nach London und durfte die Band als einziger Fotograf auf dem Flug von London nach Glasgow begleiten. Das war wie ein Ritterschlag, denn Glasgow war praktisch Rods »Mekka«. Hier war sein Lieblingsfußballverein zu Hause, hier in Schottland lagen die Wurzeln seiner Familie. Er selbst war zwar in London geboren, fühlte sich aber trotzdem wie ein Schotte und brachte dies mit seiner Liebe zu Celtic Glasgow und Schottenkaros bei jeder sich bietenden Gelegenheit deutlich zum Ausdruck.

Die mitreißende Live-Show der »neuen« Faces war der beste Beweis dafür, dass die Chemie zwischen Rod und der Band immer noch stimmte. Da wurde gerockt und gerollt, dass die Fetzen flogen. Besonders Rod und Ronnie, die bunten Paradiesvögel, tobten wie wild auf der Bühne herum und duellierten sich wie Gladiatoren mit Gitarre und Mikroständer, den Rod immer wieder herumwirbelte, kunstvoll wie ein Zirkusartist jonglierte und meterhoch in die Lüfte warf. Schon zweimal hatte er sich bei dieser Nummer das Nasenbein gebrochen, aber das hielt ihn nicht davon ab, immer waghalsigere Kunststücke und Stunts auszuprobieren! Rod raste nahezu ununterbrochen von einer Seite der Bühne zur anderen, wälzte sich am Boden, flirtete mit der Band und dem Publikum und brach am Schluss erschöpft zusammen, während Ron Wood, der nie ohne Zigarette im Mundwinkel spielte, seine explosiven Gitarrensoli mit hohen Luftsprüngen garnierte.

Nach dem Gig im Glasgower »Apollo« lud mich die Band zur Aftershow-Party ins luxuriöse Albany Hotel. Die Jungs machten ihrem Ruf als wilde Rock'n'Roller, die schon mal ein Hotelzimmer zerlegten, alle Ehre. Als ich in der Suite 705 eintraf, hatten sie sich bereits mit dem einen oder anderen Drink für die Fotosession in Stimmung gebracht, was dazu führte, dass vor der Kamera nur herumgealbert wurde. Die Faces zogen wilde Grimassen, verdrehten die Augen, vernebelten das »Set« mit Rauchschwaden und kippten dabei jede Menge Hochprozentiges. Wir hatten zwar viel Spaß bei dieser Session, aber als ich ein paar Tage später in der Redaktion die Fotos sichtete, traf mich beinahe der Schlag: Auf keinem einzigen Bild blickten alle fünf gleichzeitig in die Kamera!

Mitte '75 wanderte Rod mit seiner neuen Freundin Britt Ekland in die USA aus und veröffentlichte dort sein Solo-Album »Atlantic Crossing« mit dem Smash-Hit »Sailing«. Sowohl das Album als auch die Single stürmten weltweit die Charts und festigten Rods Superstar-Status. Ende 1975 schließlich gab Rod Stewart seinen Ausstieg bei den Faces bekannt, um sich voll und ganz auf seine Solokarriere zu konzentrieren.

THE MAN WITH
THE TWO FACES

After Rod Stewart rocketed to superstar status, the Faces gradually receded into the background and were practically demoted to being Rod's accompaniment when they went on tour together. Rod was constantly at the center of attention, the focus of the media and the fans' interest. Gradually musical differences developed too. Rod wanted more ballads put in the repertoire; the others wanted a heavier sound. Ronnie Lane toyed with the idea of leaving the band and Ronnie Wood was already flirting with the Rolling Stones.

In April of 1973, the Faces brought out their fourth album, titled »Ooh La La,« and shortly thereafter Ronnie Lane made good his threat and left the band. The band replaced him with Tetsu Yamauchi, from Japan, who used to play bass with Free. Tetsu brought some fresh ideas with him and even Rod promised to put more time into the band and to distinctly separate his solo ambitions from the Faces. He owned up to his »two faces« – the hard rock'n'roller and the romantic crooner.

After Tetsu joined, the Faces planned a world tour that would take them to Australia, New Zealand, Japan and Europe. I flew to London in December of 1973 and was permitted to accompany the band as the sole photographer on the flight from London to Glasgow that lead up to the tour. It was such an honor – Glasgow was practically Rod's »Mecca.« This was where his favorite soccer team was located, and Scotland was where his family came from. Although he was born in London, he still felt like a Scot and used every opportunity to show his love for Celtic Glasgow and to flaunt the Scottish tartan.

The incredible live show of the »new« Faces was proof enough that the chemistry between Rod and the band was still there. They were rockin' and rollin' like crazy. Particularly Rod and Ronnie, those flamboyant birds of paradise, raged like wild men on the stage and dueled like gladiators with the guitar and mike stand. Rod would skillfully twirl the mike stand, juggle it and throw it up in the air like a circus artiste again and again. He'd already broken his nose two times doing this stunt but that didn't stop him from trying out ever more daring tricks! Rod raced just about continuously from one side of the stage to the other, rolled around on the ground and flirted with the band and the audience only to break down in the end of exhaustion. In the meantime Ron Wood, who never played without a cigarette dangling out of the corner of his mouth, would embellish his explosive guitar solos by leaping high into the air.

After the gig in Glasgow's »Apollo,« the band invited me into the luxurious Albany Hotel for the after show party. The lads did credit to their wild rock'n'roller reputation of once in a while trashing a hotel room or two. When I arrived at Suite 705 they'd already had a few to get into the spirit for the photo session, which just resulted in them horsing around in front of the camera. The Faces made horrible faces, rolled their eyes, and fogged the »set« with clouds of smoke all the while knocking back a huge quantity of high-proof alcohol. We had a whole lot of fun during the shoot, but a few days later when I was looking over the photos in the editorial office I just about had a heart attack – not one of the photos showed the five of them all looking into the camera at the same time!

In the summer of 1975, Rod emigrated to the USA with his girlfriend Britt Ekland and brought out his solo album »Atlantic Crossing« with his smash hit »Sailing.« The album as well as the single stormed the charts all over the world to confirm Rod's superstar status. At the end of that year Rod Stewart officially announced his split with the Faces so that he could fully concentrate on his solo career.

DER HERZENSBRECHER

Rod war und ist ein absoluter Heartbreaker. Heerscharen von Groupies, Models, Schauspielerinnen, eine Prinzessin und sogar US-Präsidententochter Susan Ford erlagen seinem Charme.

Eine seiner Weggefährtinnen war die schöne schwedische Schauspielerin Britt Ekland, die Rod 1974 auf einer Party in Los Angeles kennen lernte. Britt hatte in der Rolle der Mary Goodnight in dem James-Bond-Kinofilm »The Man With The Golden Gun« Agent 007 alias Roger Moore und Millionen von Männern auf der ganzen Welt den Kopf verdreht. Außerdem hatte sie eine Rolle in dem Kult-Thriller »The Wicker Man« (1973) gespielt. Bevor sie Rod traf, war sie die Geliebte von Warren Beatty, Ryan O'Neal und Peter Sellers gewesen, der sie schon eine Woche nach der ersten Begegnung vom Fleck weg heiratete. Die Ehe hielt allerdings nicht lange.

Rod und Britt waren unzertrennlich. Sie begleitete ihn auf Schritt und Tritt, kümmerte sich um seine Outfits und achtete darauf, dass Rod auf der Bühne und vor der Kamera eine gute Figur machte. Er legte großen Wert auf ihr Urteil und ließ sich in Stylingfragen gerne von ihr beraten – insbesondere bei TV-Auftritten und Fototerminen.

Ich traf Britt zum ersten Mal bei der Aufzeichnung der TV-Show »Disco« in Hamburg, wo ich wie immer eines der Fernsehstudios nebenan gemietet und zu einem Fotostudio umdekoriert hatte. Zwischen den endlosen Proben kamen die Stars gerne zu mir, um sich fotografieren zu lassen – und um von meinem Büfett zu naschen, das ich extra aufgebaut hatte. Ich hatte wie immer feinste Leckereien und Champagner organisiert. Da konnte die Kantine des TV-Senders natürlich nicht mithalten! (Um die Wahrheit zu sagen: Es war natürlich kein richtiger Champagner, der die Stars ein bisschen in Stimmung brachte, sondern meine damalige Hausmarke: Henkell Trocken. Wie man deutlich auf den Fotos erkennen kann, traf ich damit trotzdem Rods erlesenen Geschmack!)

Britt und ich lagen sofort auf einer Wellenlänge, als sich per Zufall herausstellte, dass ich einen Tag nach ihr geboren wurde! Sie hatte viel Spaß bei der Fotosession und kam so richtig in Fahrt. So sehr, dass sie mich mittendrin fragte, ob sie nicht meine Assistentin werden könne! Ich fühlte mich natürlich sehr geschmeichelt und sagte erfreut zu, sie vom Fleck weg zu engagieren. Daraufhin grinste sie spitzbübisch und meinte: »Mind you – I only fly Concorde!« (»Pass auf, ich fliege aber nur mit der Concorde!«)

Schade! Damit platzten meine kühnsten Träume wie eine Seifenblase. Ich gestehe, ich hätte Britt Ekland damals nicht nur gerne als Assistentin gehabt ...

Bei einem anderen Fototermin in einer Hotelsuite in Bremen anlässlich der Aufzeichnung der TV-Show »Musikladen« fragte ich Rod, ob etwas dran sei an dem Gerücht, dass er Heiratspläne schmiede. Daraufhin brüllte Rod quer durch die Suite zu Britt, die sich im Schlafzimmer nebenan aufhielt, in breitestem Londoner Cockney-Akzent: »Daaaaarling? Are we getting married?«

Britts Antwort kam klar und unmissverständlich durch die geschlossene Tür: »F*** off!!!« (Verpiss dich!)

Die turbulente Beziehung zwischen Rod und Britt dauerte rund drei Jahre. Für sie schrieb Rod den Hit »You're In My Heart (The Final Acclaim)«, und bei dem Song »Tonight's The Night« flüstert sie leise im Hintergrund. Rod und Britt waren das schillerndste Traumpaar im Musikbusiness und füllten jahrelang die Klatschspalten der Yellow Press.

THE HEARTBREAKER

Rod was and is an absolute heartbreaker. Herds of groupies, models, actresses, a princess and even the president's daughter Susan Ford succumbed to his charms.

One of his companions was the beautiful Swedish actress Britt Ekland, who Rod had met at a party in Los Angeles in 1974. Britt turned the heads of millions of men all over the world as well as Agent 007 alias Roger Moore with her portrayal of Mary Goodnight in the James Bond film »The Man With The Golden Gun.« She also had a role in the cult thriller »The Wicker Man« (1973). Before she met Rod she had been Warren Beatty's, Ryan O'Neal's and Peter Sellers' lover respectively. Peter Sellers married her a week after meeting her. But the marriage did not last long.

Rod and Britt were inseparable. She followed him like a puppy, took care of his wardrobe and made sure that Rod looked good on stage and in front of the camera. He respected her judgment and took her advice concerning style – especially during TV appearances and photo shoots.

I met Britt for the first time during the recording for the TV show »Disco« in Hamburg. I had, as always, rented the neighboring television studio and converted it into a photo studio. The stars liked to come to me between the endless rehearsals to get photographed – and to grab a bite from the buffet that I had especially arranged for. I had, as always, the best delicacies and champagnes. Naturally the television studio canteen could not come anywhere close to my spread! (To tell you the truth, it wasn't real French champagne that put the stars in the right mood, but my own favorite brand at the time: Henkell Trocken. As can be seen from the photographs, I nevertheless met Rod's exquisite taste!)

Britt and I immediately realized we were on the same wavelength when we found out quite coincidently that I was born one day after she was born! She had a lot of fun during the photo shoot and we really got along. So much so that right in the middle of the shoot she asked me if she could become my assistant! Naturally I felt very flattered and gladly agreed to hire her on immediately. At this she grinned and roguishly said, »Mind you – I only fly Concorde!«

What a shame! My wildest dreams popped like a soap bubble. I have to confess; I would have wanted Britt Ekland for more than just her assistance...

During another photo shoot in a hotel suite in Bremen for the TV show »Musikladen,« I asked Rod if there was any truth to the rumor that he was planning on getting married. At that Rod roared to Britt in the bedroom at the other end of the suite in his broadest London Cockney, »Daaaaarling? Are we getting married?«

Britt's answer came loud and clear through the closed door »F*** off!!!«

The turbulent relationship between Rod and Britt lasted about three years. Rod wrote the hit »You're In My Heart (The Final Acclaim)« for her, and in the song »Tonight's The Night« you can hear her whispering in the background. Rod and Britt were the most dazzling couple in music business and filled the gossip pages of the yellow press for years.

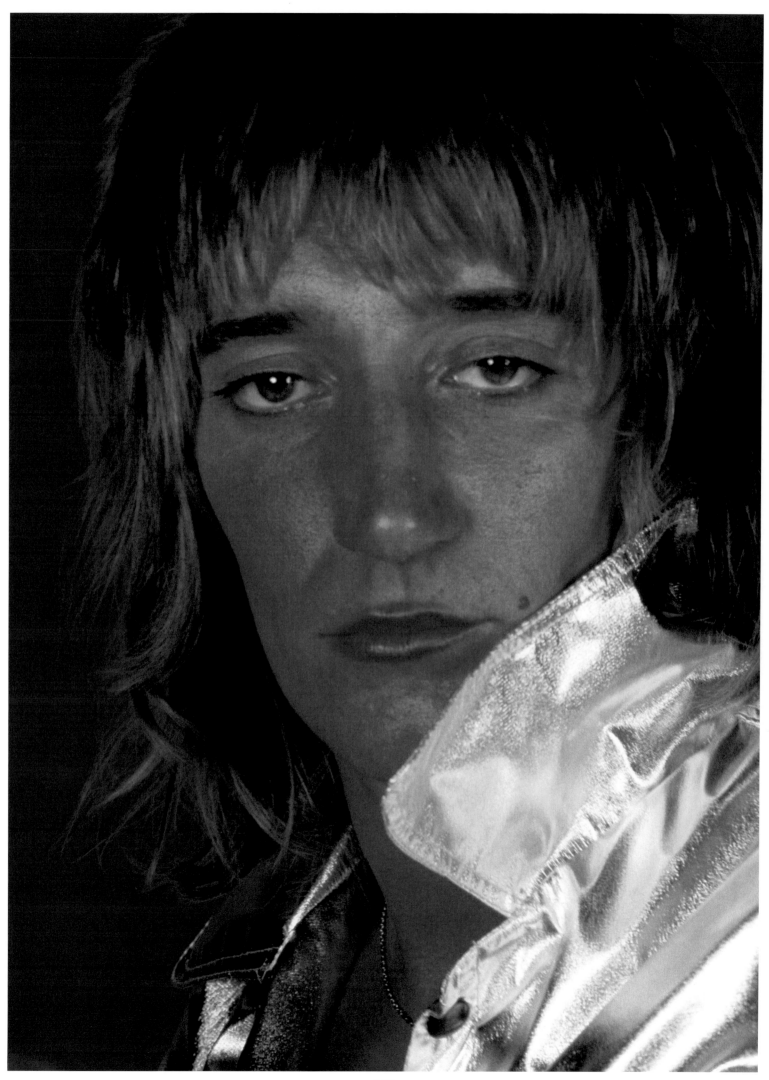

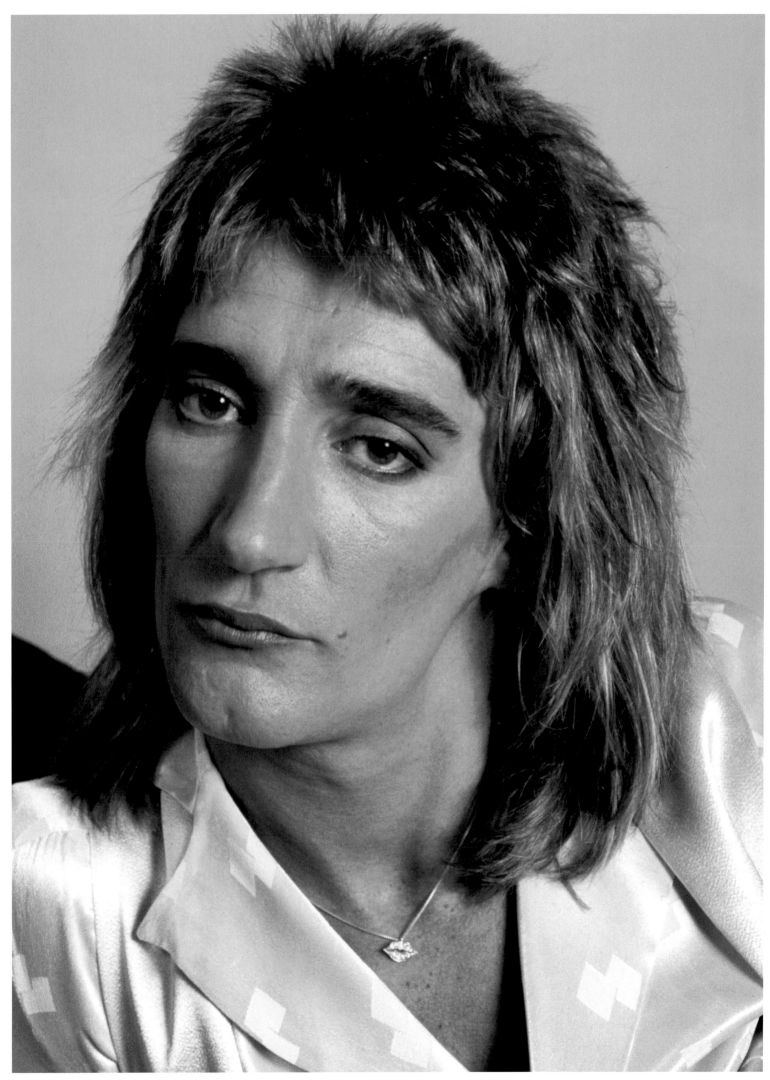

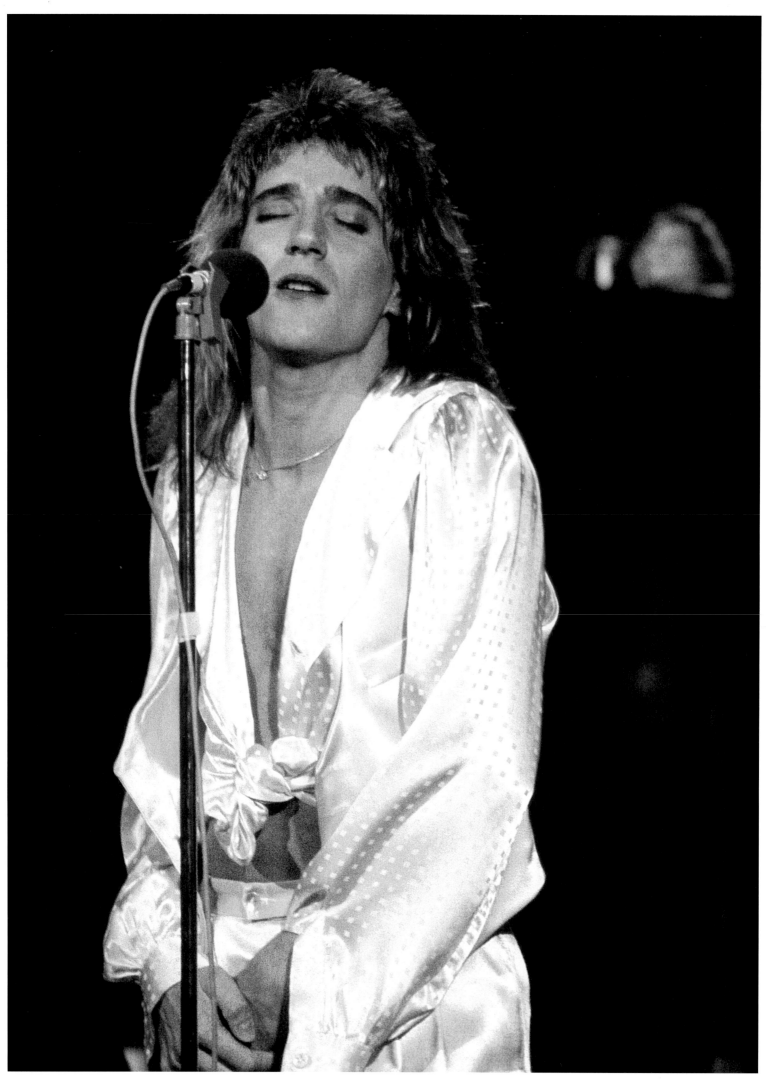

119

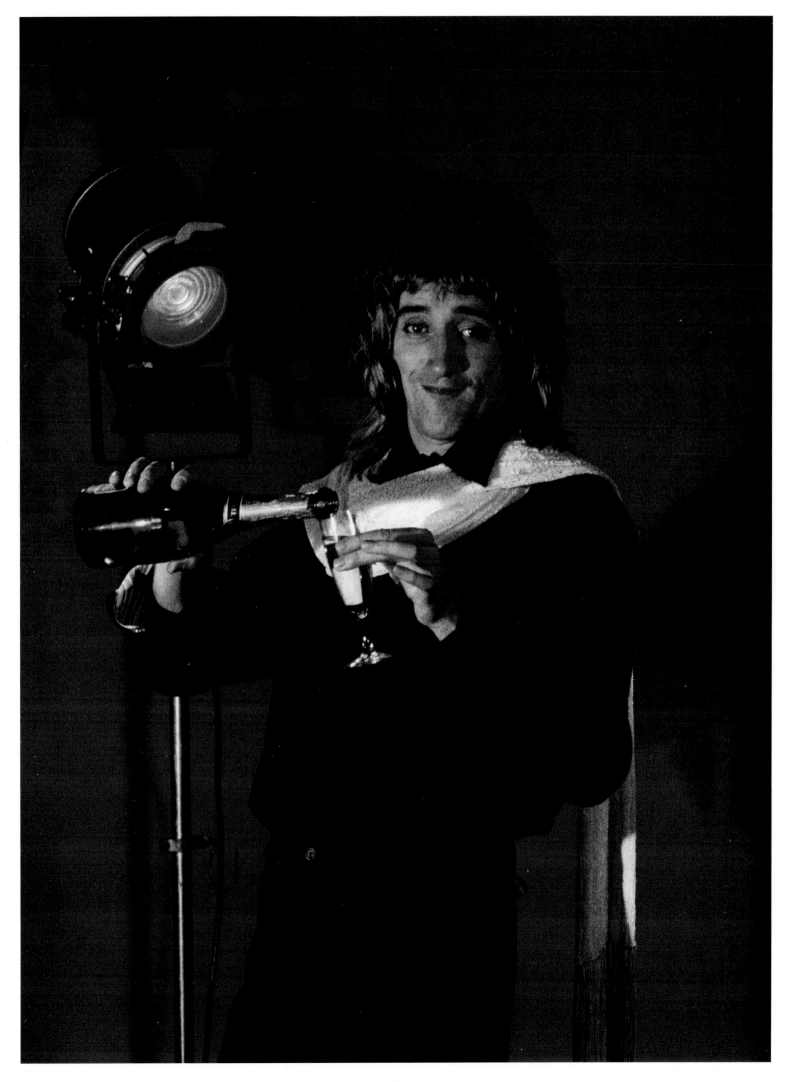

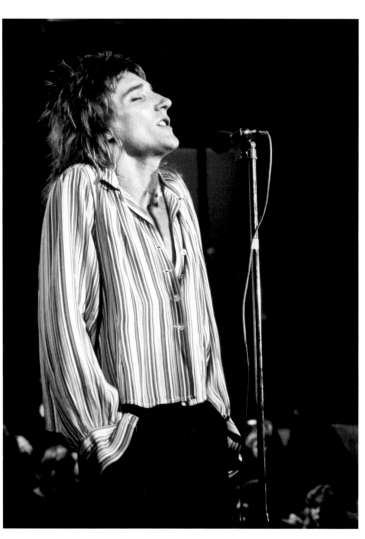

NEUANFANG

Nach der Trennung von den Faces hatte Rod beinahe zwei Jahre lang keine Bühnenluft mehr geschnuppert. Jetzt war er wieder heiß auf Live-Gigs, die für ihn so wichtig waren wie die Luft zum Atmen.

Rod gründete seine eigene Band und engagierte dafür nur absolute Top-Musiker: Gitarrist Garry Grainger von den Shadows, Chuck Berrys Gitarrist Billy Peek, Philip Chen aus Jamaika, der früher bei Jeff Beck und Donovan den Bass gezupft hatte, Organist John Jarvis (Ex-Simon & Garfunkel) und Ex-Vanilla-Fudge-Drummer Carmine Appice.

Rods erster Live-Gig nach der Trennung von den Faces: Manchester, Kings Hall. Ich war als »offizieller Tourfotograf« eingeladen und traf Rod vor der Show hinter der Bühne, um ihm »toi, toi, toi« zu wünschen. Rod war ziemlich nervös: 24 Stunden vor der Premiere musste er sich noch einer Nasen-OP unterziehen, und erst eine Stunde vor Showbeginn trafen mit Verspätung die maßgefertigten Bühnenklamotten von Designer Fiorucci aus Italien ein.

Britt Ekland wuselte backstage in der Garderobe herum und versuchte, Ordnung in das Chaos zu bringen und Rod zu besänftigen, der nervös herumtänzelte und dabei beinahe einen Fußball ins Büfett schoss.

Rod war übrigens einer der ersten Popstars, die das glamouröse Backstage-Catering kultivierten. Zu Beginn seiner Karriere reichte es, wenn ein paar Dosen Bier hinter der Bühne bereitstanden, später warteten opulente Büfetts mit leckersten Köstlichkeiten und alles, was das Herz eines jeden Barkeepers höher schlagen ließe, auf Rod und seine Band. Bei einem seiner Konzerte ließ er einmal 500 Flaschen Champagner und Sandwiches unter den Zuschauern verteilen, nachdem er sich ein bisschen verspätet hatte ... Aber diesmal blieben Champagner und Lachshäppchen unberührt, das Lampenfieber hinter der Bühne hatte nicht nur Rod, sondern auch seine Band ergriffen. Würden die Fans Rod auch ohne die Faces die Treue halten?

Das Konzert startete mit dem Song »Three Time Loser«.

Rod wirbelte in einem knallroten pyjamaartigen Satin-Anzug ausgelassen über die Bühne und servierte dem begeisterten Publikum einen prickelnden Mix aus alten und neuen Hits. Höhepunkt des Konzerts war Rods Megahit »Sailing«, bei dem ein Meer von Feuerzeugen aufleuchtete und alle mitsangen. Da bekam sogar ich Gänsehaut!

THE ROD STEWART GROUP: Garry Grainger (Gitarre), Billy Peek (Gitarre), Jim Cregan (Gitarre), Philip Chen (Bass), John Jarvis (Orgel), Carmine Appice (Schlagzeug)

A NEW BEGINNING

After leaving the Faces, Rod took an almost two year leave of absence from the stage. Now he longed to play live again, it was as important to him as the air to breathe.

Rod hired only the best musicians and put together his own band: guitarist Garry Grainger of the Shadows, Chuck Berry's guitarist Billy Peek, Philip Chen from Jamaica, who used to play bass with Jeff Beck and Donovan, organist John Jarvis (ex-Simon & Garfunkel), and ex-Vanilla Fudge drummer Carmine Appice.

Rod's first live gig after splitting with the Faces was at the King's Hall in Manchester. I was invited as the »official tour photographer« and met Rod before the show backstage to wish him luck. Rod was extremely nervous – just 24 hours before the premiere he had had another nasal operation and only one hour before the show his custom-designed stage clothes from designer Fiorucci arrived late from Italy.

Britt Ekland rummaged around in the dressing room backstage and tried to straighten out the chaos and calm Rod down, who was nervously dancing around and just about kicked a ball into the buffet table.

By the way, Rod was one of the first pop stars who cultivated gourmet backstage catering. At the beginning of his career it was enough to have a few beers ready and waiting behind the stage, later opulent buffets with the most sumptuous delicacies and anything a bartender could wish for was waiting for Rod and his band. At one of his concerts he gave out 500 bottles of champagne and sandwiches to the audience as an apology for his being late for the concert. But this time the champagne and smoked salmon remained untouched; not only Rod was struck by stage fright, the whole band was affected. Would the fans still be true to Rod even without the Faces?

The concert opened with the song »Three Time Loser.« Ron whirled energetically around on the stage in a fire-engine red pajama-like satin suit and presented his enthusiastic audience with a thrilling mix of old and new hits. The highlight of the concert was Rod's mega hit »Sailing« which inspired the audience to light up their lighters and sing along. Even I got goose bumps!

THE ROD STEWART GROUP: Garry Grainger (guitar); Billy Peek (guitar); Jim Cregan (guitar); Philip Chen (bass); John Jarvis (organ); Carmine Appice (drums)

DIE LEIDENSCHAFT

Rod Stewart ist ein absoluter Fußballfan. Er war der beste Mittelstürmer des Schulteams und wollte ursprünglich Profi-Fußballer werden. Nach der Schule trat er deshalb dem Brentwood Football Club in London bei. Nachdem er aber die ersten zwei Wochen nur die Fußballschuhe der Profis putzen durfte und kein einziges Mal eingewechselt wurde, beschloss er, seine Fußballerkarriere an den Nagel zu hängen und Popstar zu werden.

Trotzdem hatte Rod immer einen Fußball im Gepäck und spielte bei jeder sich bietenden Gelegenheit. Vor dem Soundcheck oder nach einem Konzert organisierte er oft Fußballspiele mit seiner Band und der Crew. Und zur Generalprobe bei Fernsehaufzeichnungen trägt er oft mit Stolz einen Trainingsanzug der schottischen Nationalmannschaft!

Bei seinen Shows signiert er gern Fußbälle und kickt sie ins Publikum. Inzwischen besitzt er einen eigenen Fußballplatz hinter seinem Haus in London und einen kleinen Fußballclub namens »The Vagabonds«. Und inzwischen hat er sich einen anderen großen Traum erfüllt: Bei einem Benefiz-Fußballspiel mit anderen Promis schoss er für seine Mannschaft ein Tor im Wembley-Stadion!

Rod lässt sich kein wichtiges Fußballspiel entgehen. Wo auch immer er unterwegs ist auf dieser Welt, telefoniert er mit seinem Vater, der ihm alle Ergebnisse der schottischen Liga übermittelt. Gelegentlich chartert er einen Privatjet, lädt eine Hand voll Freunde ein und düst um die halbe Welt, nur um seine Lieblingsmannschaften Celtic Glasgow, Manchester United oder die schottische Nationalmannschaft live spielen (und meist verlieren) zu sehen. Als Schottland bei der WM in Argentinien spielte, verschob er extra eine Tour. Für die Fußballweltmeisterschaft 1978 hatte Rod Stewart mit der schottischen Nationalmannschaft die Single »I'd Walk A Million Miles For One Of Your Goals« eingespielt, die sich sogar in den Top 5 der britischen Charts platzierte.

In dem Song »You're In My Heart (The Final Acclaim)«, den er für Britt Ekland schrieb (erschienen auf dem 77er Album »Foot Loose & Fancy Free«), vergleicht er seine Angebetete mit seinen Fußballclubs (»You're Celtic, United ...«) – die größte Liebeserklärung aus seinem Munde!

Vor einem Konzert in Köln hatte ich eine ganz besondere Überraschung für Rod: einen Backstage-Besuch des Nationalfußballspielers Rainer Bonhof vom deutschen Vizepokalsieger und Bundesligisten 1. FC Köln! Rod war total begeistert, als der Fußball-Weltmeister von 1974 ihm sein rotes Kölner Spielertrikot mit der Nr. 8 überreichte und erzählte, dass er am Vortag beim Bundesliga-Spiel gegen den Karlsruher SC vor 9000 Zuschauern zwei von vier Toren geschossen und damit das Spiel gewonnen hatte. Jahre später sollte Bonhof übrigens unter Berti Vogts Co-Trainer der schottischen Fußballnationalmannschaft und Coach der schottischen U21-Nationalmannschaft werden. Wahrscheinlich hat Rod ein gutes Wort für ihn eingelegt!

ROD'S PASSION

Rod Stewart is an absolute soccer fan. He was the best midfielder on his school team and originally wanted to play professional soccer. That's why he entered the London Brentwood Football Club after he left school. But after two weeks of polishing the professional players' soccer shoes and never once being sent out onto the field, he decided to hang his soccer career and become a pop star.

Nevertheless, Rod always had a soccer ball in his bags and played at every given opportunity. Before a sound check or after a concert he would often arrange a match with his band and the crew. And for a television dress rehearsal he would often proudly wear the training suit of the Scottish National Team!

At his concerts he often signed soccer balls and kicked them into the audience. In the meantime he owns his own soccer field behind his house in London and a small soccer team by the name »The Vagabonds.« And he's also fulfilled another one of his big dreams: At a benefit soccer game held in Wembley Stadium with other celebrities, he scored a goal for his team!

Rod never misses an important soccer match. Wherever he is in the world, he'll call his dad to get all the latest Scottish league scores. Sometimes he'd charter a private jet, invite a handful of his friends and jet to the other side of the world to see his favorite teams Celtic Glasgow, Manchester United or the Scottish National Team play (and usually lose) live. When Scotland played in the World Championships in Argentina he specially rearranged a tour. For the Soccer World Championships 1978 Rod Stewart recorded the single »I'd Walk A Million Miles For One Of Your Goals« with the Scottish National Team, which actually placed in the Top 5 of the British charts.

In the song »You're In My Heart (The Final Acclaim)« he wrote for Britt Ekland (appeared on the 1977 album »Foot Loose & Fancy Free«) he compared his honey to his soccer clubs (»You're Celtic, United...«) – the greatest declaration of love that would ever come out of his mouth!

Before a concert in Cologne I'd arranged a very special surprise for Rod: A backstage visit by professional player Rainer Bonhof, who played for the national league team and German cup runners-up 1. FC Köln! Rod was totally thrilled when Rainer, the soccer world champion of 1974, handed him his red Cologne team tricot with the number 8 and told him that he had played a match yesterday in the Bundesliga against the Karlsruhe SC in front of an audience of 9,000 and shot two of four goals therefore winning the match. By the way, years later Bonhof was to become co-trainer of the Scottish National Team with Berti Vogts and coach of the Scottish U21 national team. Maybe Rod put in a good word for him!

DER GESCHÄFTSMANN

Ende 1979 besuchte ich Rod mal wieder in London. Wir trafen uns im Büro seiner Plattenfirma Warner in Soho, wo sich auch ein kleines Studio befand. Dort bastelte er mit seinem Bassisten und ein paar Studiomusikern an einem neuen Song herum und führte anschließend endlose Besprechungen hinter verschlossenen Türen. Rod legte großen Wert darauf, bei den Entscheidungen für Plattencover, Promotion-Aktivitäten und Tourneeplanungen ein Wörtchen mitzureden, und so tauchte er öfter im Büro seiner Plattenfirma auf, um sich mit den Managern auszutauschen.

Rods frisch gebackene Ehefrau Alana Hamilton, Model und Ex-Frau des Schauspielers George Hamilton, die mit ihm auf dem Cover seines Hit-Albums »Blondes Have More Fun« posierte, hielt sich bescheiden im Hintergrund. Ich erwischte sie dennoch mit einem alten Fotografentrick: Ich schraubte das Weitwinkel-Objektiv auf die Kamera und tat so, als würde ich etwas anderes fotografieren. So sieht man sie auf einem der Bilder an einen Türrahmen gelehnt. Auch bei der Ankunft von Rod und Alana im schneeweißen Rolls Royce hatte ich schnell auf den Auslöser gedrückt. Auch Rod versteckte sich hinter einer riesigen Sonnenbrille – wahrscheinlich hatten die beiden die Nacht zuvor lange gefeiert!

THE BUSINESS MAN

Towards the end of 1979 I got together with Rod in London again. We met in Soho in the office of Warner Bros. Records, the company he was under contract with, which also had a small recording studio. Here he was putting together a new song with his bassist and a few studio musicians following with endless meetings behind closed doors. Rod made sure he had a say in the decision-making process for LP covers, promotions and tour planning so that he often showed up in the offices of the record company to exchange views with the managers.

Rod's new wife Alana Hamilton, the model and ex-wife of actor George Hamilton and who posed with Rod on the cover of his hit album »Blondes Have More Fun,« remained modestly in the background. Yet I caught her with an old photographer's trick: I mounted the wide-angle lens onto the camera and made as if I were photographing something else. There she is in one of the pictures leaning against the doorframe. I also managed to get a shot of them on their arrival in their snow-white Rolls Royce. Even Rod hid behind a pair of giant sunglasses – perhaps they were up too late celebrating the night before!

164

165

DER PROVOKATEUR

Kurz vor Start seiner Welttournee 1980 traf ich Rod in Bremen bei der Aufzeichnung der TV-Show »Musikladen«, wo er seinen neuen Hit »Passion« vorstellen sollte. Für diesen Auftritt hatte Rod seine Band mitgebracht. Das Bühnen-Outfit von Rod und seinen Jungs sorgte bei der Generalprobe für große Aufregung: Alle trugen schwarze T-Shirts mit der Aufschrift »SEX POLICE – It's A Thankless Task«. Das war natürlich etwas zu gewagt für das prüde deutsche Fernsehen, und so wurde vereinbart, dass diese Shirts bei der Aufzeichnung zumindest von Jacken oder Hemden verdeckt und somit »entschärft« werden sollten. Rod zog murrend seine schwarze Lederjacke und ein schwarzweiß-gemustertes Hemd über, aber während seiner Performance entledigte er sich der Jacke und knüpfte das Hemd so weit auf, dass man den »schlimmen« Spruch lesen konnte. Noch in den achtziger Jahren war so etwas ein kleiner Skandal – heute unvorstellbar!

THE AGITATOR

Shortly before his world tour in 1980, I met with Rod in Bremen during the recording for the TV show »Musikladen« where he was to introduce his new hit »Passion.« Rod brought his band with him for the performance. Rod and the band's stage clothes got everybody in a spin during the dress rehearsal. They all wore black T-shirts with the words: »SEX POLICE – It's A Thankless Task.« That was naturally too much for prudish German television and it was agreed that these shirts would be, at least for the recording, hidden by jackets or shirts and thus »defused.« Grumbling, Rod put on his black leather jacket and a black and white patterned shirt, but during his performance he took off his jacket and unbuttoned the shirt enough so that you could read the »wicked« words. That type of thing was still a bit upsetting in the '80s – unimaginable today!

175

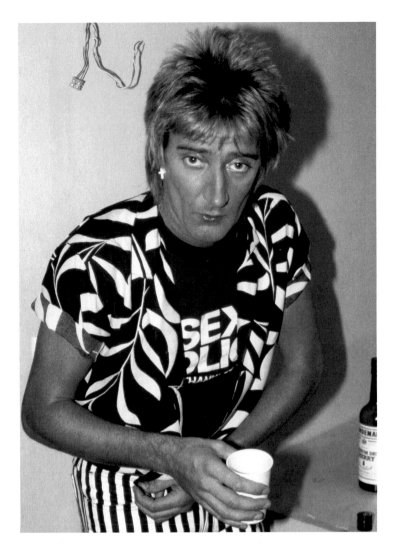

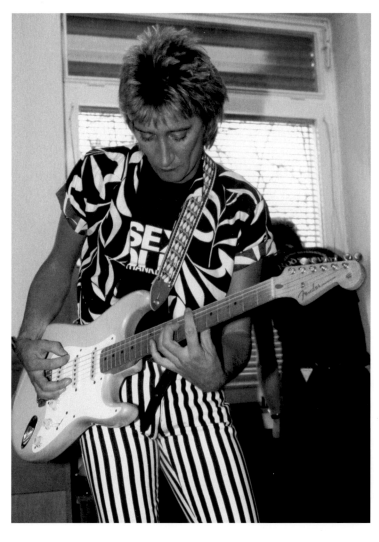

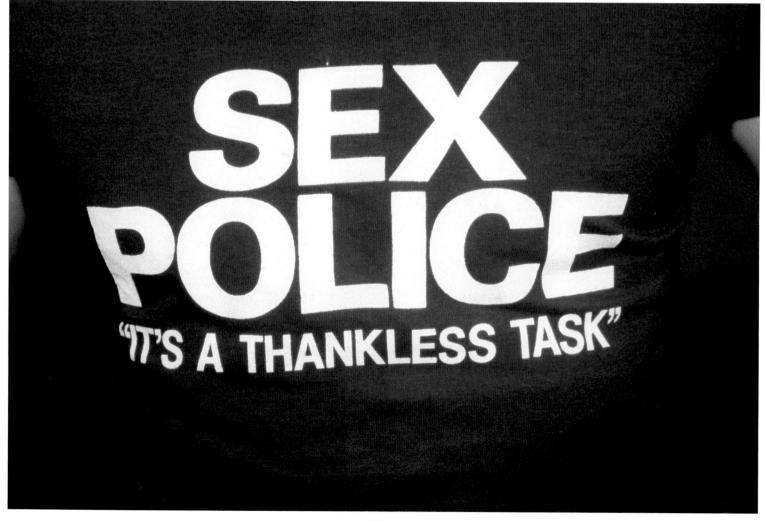

DER GEZÄHMTE

Köln, 19. Oktober 1980, Sporthalle. 3000 Fans warten seit Stunden ungeduldig vor der Halle. Zweimal schon hatte Rod Stewart seine geplante Deutschland-Tour abgesagt, jetzt war er endlich da und konnte seinen Fans beweisen, dass er trotz seiner 35 Jahre immer noch einer der heißesten Rock-Sänger der Welt war.

Ich traf Rod nachmittags backstage in seiner Garderobe, wo er sich mit Stretching und Lockerungsübungen für den Auftritt am Abend fit machte und noch mal alle Details der Show Revue passieren ließ. Rod Stewart ist ein absoluter Perfektionist und Control-Freak, der sich höchstpersönlich um jedes einzelne Detail der Show kümmerte. Nach dem Soundcheck relaxte Rod mit einem kleinen Fußballmatch in der Halle, während die Roadies noch letzte Hand anlegten bei der Bühne, die nach Rods Entwürfen extra angefertigt worden war.

Kurz vor dem Gig war Rod etwas nervös, wie die deutschen Fans ihn aufnehmen würden, nachdem er die Tour schon zweimal verschoben hatte. Aber seine Befürchtungen waren umsonst. Unter dem unbeschreiblichen Jubel der Fans stürmte Rod auf die Bühne und legte los mit »Hot Legs«. Dann schoss er ein wahres Hit-Feuerwerk ab, wechselte mehrfach sein Outfit und tobte mit seinem Mikroständer über die Bühne. Die Fans waren sich einig: Das lange Warten hatte sich gelohnt!

Nach der Show lud Rod mich zu einem Drink an der Bar im Hotel Interconti ein, wo er mit seiner Band residierte. Früher waren wilde, nächtelange Saufgelage mit seiner Band nach jeder Show an der Tagesordnung, aber offenbar hatte ihn seine Ehefrau Alana gezähmt. Rod stand gesittet an der Bar und unterhielt sich mit den Jungs von seiner Band. Zwei Mädchen, die es geschafft hatten, sich an der Security vorbei ins Hotel zu mogeln, pirschten sich an mich heran und bestürmten mich, sie mit Rod bekannt zu machen. Da ich wusste, dass er frisch verheiratet war und sicher keine Lust auf einen One-Night-Stand hatte, verriet ich ihnen Rods früheren Standard-Aufreißerspruch, mit dem er bislang jedes Mädchen herumgekriegt hatte. Wenn ihm ein Mädchen gefiel, stellte er sich höflich vor und fragte dann artig: »I guess a f*** is out of question?« (»Ich nehme mal an, dass du nicht mit mir schlafen willst, oder?«) Damit eroberte er sämtliche Groupies im Handumdrehen, aber ich bezweifle, dass Otto Normalverbraucher mit so einer Anmache Erfolg hat! Jedenfalls waren die beiden Fans total begeistert, dass ich ihnen Rods geheimes »Simsalabim« verriet. Nach einigem Gekicher und Getuschel wagten sie schließlich den Spieß umzudrehen und Rod anzusprechen. »Hi Rod! We guess a f*** is out of question?!?«

Rod Stewart, das größte Sex-Symbol der siebziger und achtziger Jahre, war absolut sprachlos. Er stellte sein Glas ab und verabschiedete sich grinsend mit den Worten: »I think I should call my wife Alana in Los Angeles. Good Night!«

Damit verschwand er blitzschnell in seinem Hotelzimmer – und zwar allein!

Kurz nach diesem Konzert hängte ich meine Kamera nach mehr als einem Jahrzehnt als Fotograf an den Nagel und wechselte in die Chefredaktion von BRAVO. Beim Durchforsten meines Foto-Archivs für diesen Bildband im Herbst 2004 – rund 35 Jahre nach unserer ersten Begegnung in London – bestätigte sich Rod Stewarts Songtitel: »Every Picture Tells A Story!« Thank you, Rod!

DEUTSCHLAND-TOUR 1980: Köln, 19.10.; Hamburg, 21.10.; Berlin, 23.10.; München, 28.10.; Frankfurt/Main, 29.10.; Bremen, 30.10.; Dortmund, 01.11.; Düsseldorf, 02.11.; Stuttgart, 04.11.

ROD STEWART BAND: Jim Cregan (Gitarre), Bill Peek (Gitarre), Gary Grainger (Gitarre), Phil Chen (Bass), Kevin Savigar (Klavier/Synthesizer), Carmine Appice (Schlagzeug)

TAMED

Cologne, October 19th 1980, Sporthalle. For hours 3,000 fans had been waiting impatiently out front. Twice Rod Stewart had cancelled his German tour, now he was finally here and could prove to his fans that despite his 35 years he was still one of the hottest rock singers in the world.

I met with Rod at noon backstage in his dressing room where he was loosening up with stretching and limbering-up exercises for the performance that evening and went over all the details of the show with him again. Rod Stewart is an absolute perfectionist and control freak, who personally takes care of every single detail in the show. After the sound check Rod relaxed with a small soccer match in the hall while the roadies finished up the stage, which was custom built to Rod's design.

Shortly before the gig Rod got a bit nervous about how the German fans would react to him after he'd already postponed the tour twice. But his fear was in vain. While the fans cheered beyond description, Rod stormed onto the stage and let it rip with »Hot Legs.« Then he let go with an out-and-out explosion of hits, repeatedly changed his outfit and dashed all over the stage with his mike stand. The feeling was unanimous – it was worth the wait!

After the show Rod invited me for a drink at the bar of the Hotel Interconti where he and the band were staying. In the old days he and the band would celebrate after every show with all-night drinking; apparently his wife Alana had tamed him. Rod was at the bar and conversed with the guys in his band in a civilized manner. Two girls who managed to get past hotel security stalked me and implored me to introduce them to Rod. Because I knew that he was newly married and certainly didn't feel like a one-night stand I revealed to them Rod's earlier standard pick-up line, the one that got every girl round. If he saw a girl he liked he'd introduce himself to her and politely ask, »I guess a f*** is out of the question?« With that line he conquered every groupie instantly, but I doubt that Joe Normal would have the same success with it! Anyway, the two fans were totally thrilled that I revealed Rod's secret »open sesame« to them. After a few giggles and a bit of fuss the two courageously decided to turn the tables and address Rod. »Hi Rod! We guess a f*** is out of question?!?«

Rod Stewart, the greatest sex symbol of the seventies and eighties, was absolutely speechless. He put down his glass and left the room grinning with the words, »I think I should call my wife Alana in Los Angeles. Good Night!«

With that he disappeared to his hotel room – alone!

Shortly after this concert I hung up my camera after more than a decade as a photographer and became the editor of BRAVO magazine. Going through my photo archive in the fall of 2004 for this photographic book – about 35 years after our first encounter in London – Rod Stewart's song title »Every Picture Tells A Story!« gets another meaning. Thank you, Rod!

GERMANY TOUR 1980: Cologne, Oct. 19; Hamburg, Oct. 21; Berlin, Oct. 23; Munich, Oct. 28; Frankfurt, Oct. 29; Bremen, Oct. 30; Dortmund, Nov. 1; Düsseldorf, Nov. 2; Stuttgart, Nov. 11

THE ROD STEWART BAND: Jim Cregan (guitar); Billy Peek (guitar); Garry Grainger (guitar); Phil Chen (bass); Kevin Savigar (plano/synthesizer); Carmine Appice (drums)

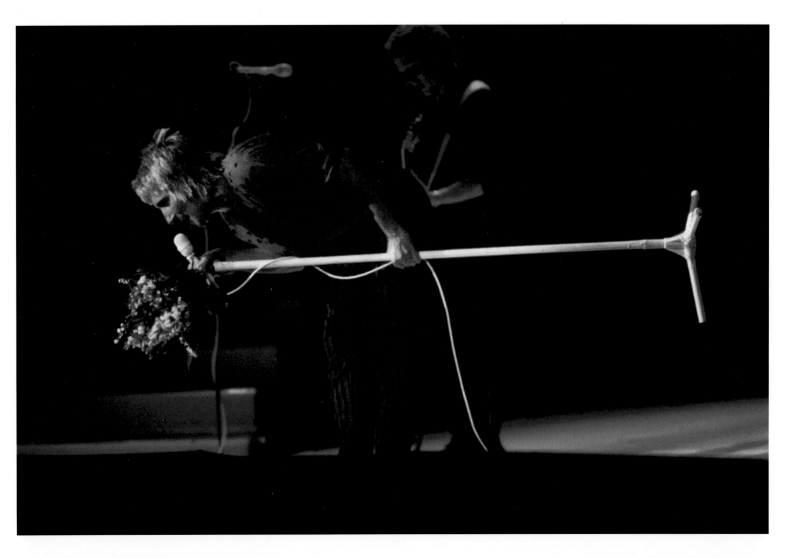

INFORMATION

Rod Stewart im Internet:
www.rodstewart.com (Official Website)
www.rod-stewart.de
www.rodstewartfanclub.com
www.rodstewartonline.com

Bubi Heilemanns Homepage: www.rockfoto.de
(Fotos von Rod Stewart u.a.)

Aktuelle Veröffentlichungen:

CD:
Rod Stewart: It Had To Be You ...
The Great American Songbook Vol. I
Rod Stewart: As Time Goes By ...
The Great American Songbook Vol. II
Rod Stewart: Stardust ...
The Great American Songbook Vol. III
CD-Box: The Faces: Five Guys Walk Into A Bar ...

DVD/VIDEO:
Rod Stewart: It Had To Be You ... The Great American Songbook
Rod Stewart: One Night Only! Live At Royal Albert Hall
Rod Stewart: Storytellers / VH1
(Alle Angaben ohne Gewähr.)

SPECIAL THANKS:
Bubi Heilemann dankt für tatkräftige Hilfe
bei diesem Buch: Sabine Thomas und Andy Hoh,
Renate Günther, Martin Twickler und
Wolferl Krüger.

Vielen Dank an das Team vom
Verlag Schwarzkopf & Schwarzkopf, besonders
Frank Wonneberg, Ulrike Bauer, Anne Litvin, Sylvie Malich,
Susan Pawlak, Radek Polák, Berit Koepke, Linn Schumacher,
Daniel Spitzer und last but not least Oliver Schwarzkopf
für sein unglaubliches Engagement!

Very Special Thanks to Rod Stewart.
Every picture tells a story!

Bubi Heilemanns Bücher erscheinen im
Verlag Schwarzkopf & Schwarzkopf.

Bisher erschienen:
ABBA (2004)
AC/DC (2004)
BAY CITY ROLLERS (2004)

Weitere Fotobände sind in Vorbereitung!
Infos unter www.schwarzkopf-schwarzkopf.de

Rod Stewart on the Internet:
www.rodstewart.com (Official Website)
www.rod-stewart.de
www.rodstewartfanclub.com
www.rodstewartonline.com

Bubi Heilemann's homepage: www.rockfoto.de
(photographs of Rod Stewart, etc.)

Current Releases:

CD:
Rod Stewart: It Had To Be You ...
The Great American Songbook Vol. I
Rod Stewart: As Time Goes By ...
The Great American Songbook Vol. II
Rod Stewart: Stardust...
The Great American Songbook Vol. III
CD Box: The Faces: Five Guys Walk Into A Bar...

DVD/VIDEO:
Rod Stewart: It Had To Be You... The Great American Songbook
Rod Stewart: One Night Only! Live At Royal Albert Hall
Rod Stewart: Storytellers / VH1
(We assume no responsibility for the
correctness of this information.)

SPECIAL THANKS:
Bubi Heilemann would like to thank the following people
for their energetic help with this book: Sabine Thomas
and Andy Hoh, Renate Günther, Martin Twickler and
Wolferl Krüger.

Many thanks to the team at
Verlag Schwarzkopf & Schwarzkopf, especially
Frank Wonneberg, Ulrike Bauer, Anne Litvin, Sylvie Malich,
Susan Pawlak, Radek Polák, Berit Koepke, Linn Schumacher,
Daniel Spitzer and, last but not least, Oliver Schwarzkopf
for his incredible dedication!

Very Special Thanks to Rod Stewart.
Every picture tells a story!

Bubi Heilemann's books are published by the
Schwarzkopf & Schwarzkopf publishing house.

Published so far:
ABBA (2004)
AC/DC (2004)
BAY CITY ROLLERS (2004)

Further photography books are in the works!
Information at: www.schwarzkopf-schwarzkopf.de.

DIE BUBI-HEILEMANN-EDITION
THE BUBI HEILEMANN SERIES

Wolfgang »Bubi« Heilemann war einer der gefragtesten Star-Fotografen der siebziger Jahre. Als Exklusiv-Fotograf für BRAVO bekam er alle Superstars dieser schillernden Epoche vor seine Linse. Heilemanns stolze Bilanz: über 250 BRAVO-Titelbilder, unzählige Poster, Plattencover und natürlich die legendären BRAVO-Starschnitte. In seinem Archiv lagern buchstäblich Millionen von Dias, darunter höchst brisante und bislang unveröffentlichte Aufnahmen von Superstars wie ABBA, AC/DC, Led Zeppelin, Beatles, Rolling Stones, Jimi Hendrix, Bee Gees, T. Rex, Sweet und vielen anderen Rock-Heroes.

Für die exklusive Bubi-Heilemann-Edition im Verlag Schwarzkopf & Schwarzkopf öffnet Heilemann sein einzigartiges Archiv. Heilemann lässt Bilder lebendig werden und erzählt die Story, die hinter dem Foto steckt. Diese hochkarätige Mischung aus erstklassigem Bildmaterial und fesselnden Storys ist das faszinierende Zeitdokument eines Insiders in Wort und Bild über die größten Superstars der Seventies.

1980 hängte Heilemann seine Kamera an den Nagel und wechselte in die Chefredaktion von BRAVO. Später ging er als Regisseur zum Fernsehen, wo er Musiksendungen (»BRAVO-TV«, »FORMEL EINS«, »TEEN-MAGAZIN«) und diverse Features für die ARD drehte. Nebenbei eröffnete er in München Deutschlands ersten Karaoke-Shop.

Heilemanns erster Fotoband »ABBA – Photographien 1974–1980«, erschienen im Frühjahr 2004 in der Edition Bubi Heilemann bei Schwarzkopf & Schwarzkopf, schlug ein wie eine Granate und stürmte die Bestsellerlisten, gefolgt von Bildbänden über die Bay City Rollers und AC/DC. Der Fotoband über Rod Stewart setzt die erfolgreiche Reihe fort. Weitere Bände sind bereits in Vorbereitung.

Bubi Heilemanns Co-Autorin Sabine Thomas wurde bekannt als TV-Moderatorin von Musiksendungen (»MUSICBOX« u. a.), DJane, Musikredakteurin und Drehbuch- und Krimi-Autorin.

Wolfgang »Bubi« Heilemann was one of the most sought-after photographers of stars and celebrities of the seventies. All the stars of this glittering decade landed, sooner or later, in front of the camera lens of Heilemann, who worked exclusively for BRAVO. At the end of his career as professional photographer, he could proudly lay claim to over 250 BRAVO cover-shots, posters too numerous to count, album-covers, and, of course, the legendary BRAVO »Star Cuts«. Stored away in his photo archive are literally millions of slides, some of them explosive but as yet unpublished shots of such superstars as ABBA, AC/DC, Led Zeppelin, The Beatles, The Rolling Stones, Jimi Hendrix, The Bee Gees, T. Rex, The Bay City Rollers, and The Sweet along with many other rock heroes.

For the exclusive »Bubi Heilemann Series« published by Schwarzkopf & Schwarzkopf, Heilemann has opened this unique archive. Heilemann not only lets the picture speak its »thousand words« but relates the story behind the photograph. This jaw-dropping combination of high-class photo material and riveting stories is the intriguing document of an insider, in words and pictures, about the greatest superstars of the seventies.

In 1980, Heilemann »hung up his camera« and joined the senior editorial staff of BRAVO. Later, he worked in television as a director for music programs (»BRAVO-TV,« »FORMEL EINS,« »TEEN-MAGAZIN«) and various other features for the TV channel ARD. Besides all these activities, he somehow also found time to open Germany's first karaoke shop in Munich.

The first publication of Heilemann's photos in book form, »ABBA – Photographs 1974–1980«, appeared in spring 2004 in Schwarzkopf & Schwarzkopf's Bubi Heilemann Series. Its success with the reading public was huge and immediate and it shot to the top of the best-seller lists, followed by books about the Bay City Rollers and AC/DC. This book of photos and texts, which focuses on Rod Stewart, is a continuation of this successful series. Further volumes are already in preparation.

Bubi Heilemann's co-author Sabine Thomas made her name as a presenter of TV music programs (amongst others »MUSICBOX«), as a DJane, as an editor of music magazines and as an author of screenplays and detective novels.

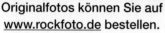

Originalfotos können Sie auf
www.rockfoto.de bestellen.

Original photos are available at
www.rockfoto.de.

IMPRESSUM

Wolfgang »Bubi« Heilemann:
ROD STEWART
LIVE | PRIVATE | BACKSTAGE – PHOTOS 1970-1980
ISBN 3-89602-647-X

Bildredaktion & Gesamtgestaltung: Frank Wonneberg
Übersetzung: Sylvie Malich, Berlin
Retusche und Bildbearbeitung: Susan Pawlak, Radek Polák,
Berit Koepke, Linn Schumacher

Katalog
Wir senden Ihnen gern unseren kostenlosen Katalog.
Schwarzkopf & Schwarzkopf Verlag GmbH / Abt. Service
Kastanienallee 32, 10435 Berlin
Telefon: 030 – 44 33 63 00
Fax: 030 – 44 33 63 044

Internet
www.schwarzkopf-schwarzkopf.de

E-Mail
info@schwarzkopf-schwarzkopf.de